COPYRIGHT

Copyright 2023 by ScissorTale Publishing LLC

All rights reserved.

No part of this publication may be reproduced, distributed, or transmitted in any form or by any means, including photocopying, recording, or other electronic or mechanical methods, without the prior written permission of the publisher, except as permitted by U.S. copyright law. For permission requests, contact ScissorTale Publishing LLC.

The story, all names, characters, and incidents portrayed in this production are fictitious. No identification with actual persons (living or deceased), places, buildings, and products is intended or should be inferred.

ISBN
979-8-9882121-1-9

A PARABLE SHAREABLES Story

In honor of the phrase

"The grass is always greener on the other side"

adapted from the original

"The harvest is always richer in another man's field." —Ovid

Daisy Dulas

Finds the Best Grass

MJ LITTLE

In the heart of South Africa,
on a farm green and vast

Lived a happy sweet cow,
named Daisy Dulas.

One day as she hummed
just the happiest tune,
she glanced towards the hills
past the creek by the dune.

Then the sun cast a ray,
bright as she'd ever seen,
toward the wildland savannah
where the grass looked so green.

Daisy stood slack-jawed,
locked in on the scene,
"Wild grass looks delicious,
I hereby decree."

Then Daisy said smugly
as she choked down her bite,
"I've been eating this bland grass
both day and night."

"I can't see myself eating
this slop all my life,
if I ate that wild grass
I'd be filled with delight."

She spoke to her friends,
and they saw and agreed,
they'd go to the wild bush,
where the grass looked so green.

Then they hatched a quick plan to sneak out that night...

AND GO ON THIS GRAND JOURNEY

BY THE MOON'S LIGHT.

So they slipped through the fence
and then ran out to see,
the grass wasn't as green
as they thought it would be.

Just then a loud roar
pierced through the dark night,
and a pride of young lions
right froze them with fright.

Daisy wished she was back
at the farm with the gate,
where the grass was delicious
from morning til' late.

"Dinner's gonna be easy,
prepare for a feast!,"
said the fierce mother lion
as they sharpened their teeth.

And right when it seemed
all would come to an end,
the voice of their farmer
rang aloud from the bend.

The lions were startled,
and they fled the scene fast,

While sweet Daisy and friends were saved at long last.

Daisy learned a true lesson
that made lots of sense,
The grass isn't greener
on that side of the fence.

So before crossing fences
that ought not be crossed,
learn to value what's yours
and don't count it as loss.

Made in United States
North Haven, CT
18 January 2024

47612728R00024